D0793756

INDIVIDUAL SPORTS
OF THE
SUMMER GAMES

Aaron Derr

RED
CHAIR
· PRESS ·

Gold Medal Games is produced and published by Red Chair Press:

Red Chair Press LLC   PO Box 333   South Egremont, MA 01258-0333

www.redchairpress.com

Publisher's Cataloging-In-Publication Data

Names: Derr, Aaron, author. | Sperling, Thomas, 1952- illustrator.

Title: Individual sports of the Summer Games / Aaron Derr ; [illustrations by Thomas Sperling].

Description: South Egremont, MA : Red Chair Press, [2020] | Series: Gold medal games | Interest age level: 007-010. | Includes bibliographical references and index. | Summary: "An overview of the modern Olympic Games featuring sports played by individual athletes competing against each other ... These athletes compete in more than 300 events. The games showcase the strength and skills, stamina and endurance of amazing individual athletes from around the world."--Provided by publisher.

Identifiers: ISBN 9781634407205 (library hardcover) | ISBN 9781634407250 (paperback) | ISBN 9781634407304 (ebook)

Subjects: LCSH: Olympics--Juvenile literature. | Individual sports--Juvenile literature. | CYAC: Olympics. | Sports.

Classification: LCC GV721.53 .D47 2020 (print) | LCC GV721.53 (ebook) | DDC 796.48--dc23

LCCN: 2018963383

Illustrations by Thomas Sperling.

Photo credits: Cover, pp. 1–9, 13, 16–19, 21 (bottom), 22, 24–28, 30–32, 35–38, 42, 44, 45 (top) Shutterstock; p. 10 © Hulton Archive/Getty Images; p. 11 (top, bottom) © Getty Images; p. 12 © The History Collection/Alamy; pp. 14–15 © RooM the Agency/Alamy; p.15 © Photofusion Picture Library/Alamy; pp. 20, 29, 33, 39, 43 © PA Images/Alamy; p. 21 (top) © PCN Photography/Alamy; p. 23 (top) © ZUMA Press, Inc./Alamy; p. 23 (bottom) © Diane Johnson/Alamy; p. 34 © AF archive/Alamy; p. 40 © Luiz Souza/Alamy; p. 41 © Aflo Co., Ltd./Alamy; 45 (center) © Action Plus Sports Images/Alamy; p. 45 (bottom) Dreamstime.

Printed in the United States of America

0320 2P CGS20

TABLE OF CONTENTS

THE SUMMER GAMES

The opening ceremony is a big, colorful celebration.

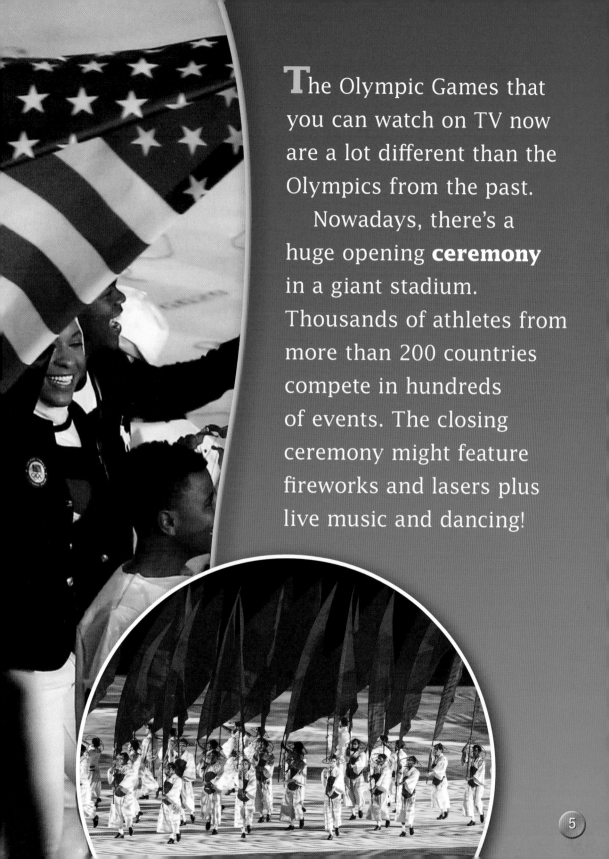

The Olympic Games that you can watch on TV now are a lot different than the Olympics from the past. Nowadays, there's a huge opening **ceremony** in a giant stadium. Thousands of athletes from more than 200 countries compete in hundreds of events. The closing ceremony might feature fireworks and lasers plus live music and dancing!

But it hasn't always been like this. In fact, the Olympics began so long ago that it's difficult to know exactly why and how they started in the first place! Most experts believe that the first Games happened in 776 BC in an area of Greece called Olympia.

The games honored Zeus, the king of gods.

This was the beginning of what is now called the **ancient** Olympic Games. These first Olympics were a celebration in honor of Zeus, the king of the gods in the ancient Greek religion. The games were held every four years, a period of time called an Olympiad.

Back then, hundreds of athletes competed in sports such as horse and **chariot** racing, running, wrestling and boxing. Thanks to something called the Olympic Truce, the athletes were able to travel safely to and from the Games. This was important because often their countries were at war with each other!

The Olympic Truce has been used to allow athletes from North Korea and South Korea to compete as one team. They are still at war with each other.

There were no gold, silver or bronze **medals** in the ancient Olympics. There were no team sports, either. Each event had only one winner, and his reward was a **wreath** or crown made from leaves. It might not sound like much now, but it was considered a great honor back then!

The Games continued like this for more than 1,000 years, until they were **banned** by Emperor Theodosius I in 393 AD. Theodosius was a Christian, and he didn't approve of any celebrations for Zeus or other Greek gods.

Athletes in the ancient games competed without clothing.

Olympics Reborn!

In 1894, an idea was born to restart the Olympic Games. A Frenchman named Pierre de Coubertin founded the **International** Olympic Committee (IOC). The IOC is a group of volunteers that serve as the authority of the modern Olympic Games.

The 1896 Olympic stadium in Athens, Greece

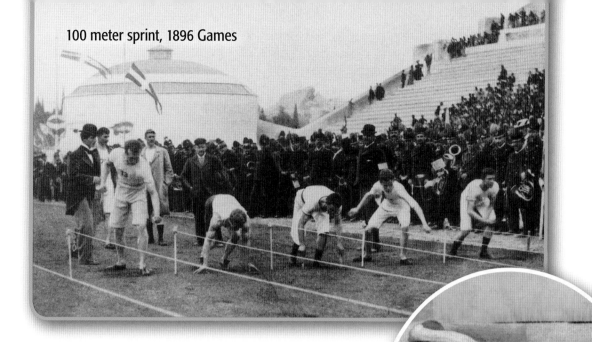

100 meter sprint, 1896 Games

The first modern Games were held in Athens, Greece, in 1896. They featured 241 athletes from 14 different countries competing in 43 sporting events. German athlete Carl Schuhmann led the way with four individual first-place finishes. The United States had the most first-place finishes with 11.

Robert Garrett, USA, 1896 gold medalist

The 1896 Olympics were a huge success. At the time, it was the biggest international sporting event ever held and featured the largest crowds ever known to watch a sporting event. The Olympics were back!

The Tradition Continues

Since 1896, the Summer Olympics have been held every four years, with three **exceptions**. In 1916, the Olympics were called off because of World War I. And in 1940 and 1944, the Olympics were canceled due to World War II.

The event has gotten a lot bigger. There are now more than 300 events and more than 10,000 competitors from more than 200 nations.

In March 2020, the Summer Games in Tokyo were rescheduled for 2021 due to a worldwide pandemic.

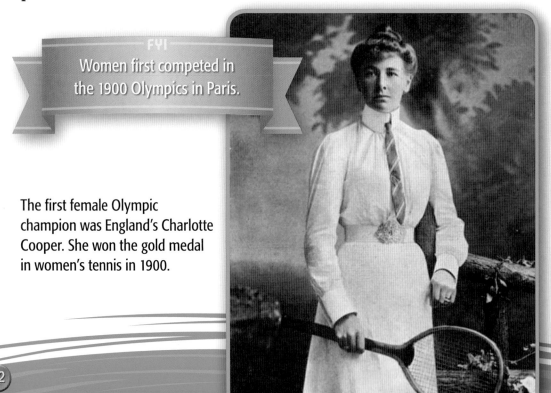

FYI
Women first competed in the 1900 Olympics in Paris.

The first female Olympic champion was England's Charlotte Cooper. She won the gold medal in women's tennis in 1900.

Thomas Bach, IOC president, speaks at Rio 2016 Games.

The United States Olympic Committee (USOC) helps decide who gets to go to the Olympics from the United States. American athletes work long and hard to try to qualify for the Olympics. Most of them have been competing in their sport since they were little kids!

Some sports have competitions called Olympic Trials that feature the best American athletes in each sport competing against each other to decide who gets to go to the Olympic Games. These competitions are super tough. Everybody wants to make it to the Olympics!

Beijing Olympic Stadium

Gold Medal Cities

The Summer Olympics are hosted by a different city every four years. Here is a list of the host cities for the most recent Summer Games, plus some that haven't even happened yet. The IOC really likes to plan ahead!

2028: Los Angeles	2004: Athens	1980: Moscow
2024: Paris	2000: Sydney	1976: Montreal
2020: Tokyo (2021)*	1996: Atlanta	1972: Munich
2016: Rio de Janeiro	1992: Barcelona	1968: Mexico City
2012: London	1988: Seoul	1964: Tokyo
2008: Beijing	1984: Los Angeles	1960: Rome

*The 2020 Games in Tokyo were rescheduled to 2021 due to the pandemic.

ATHLETICS, GYMNASTICS AND AQUATICS

Scenes from the 2016 Summer
Games in Rio de Janeiro

Events such as the 100-meter dash, marathon, relay races, high jump, shot put and decathlon are grouped together in the Olympics under the name "Athletics." They are some of the most popular sports in all of the Olympic Games. Everybody loves athletics!

Each athletic event requires a different skill. The 100-meter dash is a sprint race. It is a test of speed. In fact, the winner is often called "the fastest person in the world."

The marathon, on the other hand, requires participants to run 26 miles (42 kilometers). It's a test of **endurance** and **stamina**.

The high jump and long jump test jumping ability. The shot put and discus throw are tests of strength. The 4 X 100 (pronounced "4 by 100") requires four athletes to each do their part in a **relay** race. And the decathlon is a combination of 10 different events, each with their own unique demands.

Women's long jump:
Australia's Brooke Stratton

Men's shot put: USA's
Ryan Crouser

Women's marathon:
Rio Olympics 2016.

One of the most inspiring moments in Olympic history came in the 1992 Barcelona Olympics when British athlete Derek Redmond was injured during the 400-meter dash. Even though he could barely walk, Derek, with help from his father, limped to the finish line. He was determined to finish the race.

"I decided I was going to finish that race if it was the last race I ever did," Redmond said.

Great Britain's Derek Redmond and his father

Pommel horse event:
USA's Daniel Leyva

USA's
Simone Biles

Gymnastics

Like athletics, gymnastics has
been a part of every modern
Olympic Summer Games. The
most popular gymnastics events
are called artistic gymnastics.
Athletes perform short routines at
different stations with different equipment.
They are graded by judges, and the athletes
with the best combined scores are the winners.

Artistic gymnastics include a floor exercise, a bar routine and a vault. Women's gymnasts also compete on the balance beam, while men do a pommel horse and rings routine. The balance beam is only a few inches wide, and the gymnasts do all kinds of jumps, twists and spins on the beam!

Rhythmic gymnastics are like ballet and dance. They were introduced at the 1984 Olympics. In 2000, trampoline events were added. These are super fun to watch because the athletes fly sky high!

Rhythmic gymnastics: Bulgaria's Neviana Vladinova

One of the most important Americans in gymnastics history is Mary Lou Retton. In 1984 Retton became the first American to win the Olympic gymnastics all-around title. She earned a perfect score in the vault and immediately became a huge **celebrity**.

"For athletes, the Olympics are the ultimate test of their worth," Retton said.

A **decade** later, Shannon Miller earned seven medals in the 1992 and 1996 Games, more than any other American gymnast had ever earned. And two decades after that, in 2016, Simone Biles earned four gold medals, an American record for most gold medals in women's gymnastics at a single Olympic Games.

JUST JOKING

Q: What's a banana's favorite gymnastics move?

A: The splits!

Simone Biles (left), and Aly Raisman (right)

Women's 200 meter individual medley: USA's Maya Dirado (right)

Aquatics

Just like athletics and gymnastics, swimming has been a sport at every modern Olympics. The 100-meters freestyle is the most popular event. It's called freestyle because the competitors can choose whichever stroke style they want. And they can swim fast, too!

Other races require swimmers to use a certain stroke, such as the backstroke, the breaststroke, or the butterfly. A medley race consists of swimmers rotating through the different styles during the same race. A relay race has four swimmers taking turns and racing as a team.

Synchronized swimming splashed onto the Olympic scene in 1984. Also called artistic swimming, it's not a race. It is like a floor routine in gymnastics.

Diving is the sport of jumping into a pool from a high diving board, then performing stunts and acrobatics on the way down. The divers twist and turn and spin but always enter the water with their hands first and their bodies straight up and down!

10 meter platform diving

USA's Michael Phelps

USA's Katie Ledecky

Two of the most **accomplished** swimmers in the world are from the United States. Michael Phelps has earned 28 medals, the most of any Olympian in any sport. And Katie Ledecky was the most decorated female athlete in the 2016 Olympics, with four gold medals, one silver medal and two world records.

"When I was little I never dreamed of going to the Olympics, but once I got there I wanted to do my very best at that level," Ledecky said.

CHAPTER 3

Cycling, Tennis and Shooting Sports

Men's Road Cycling: Rio 2016 Games

The sport of cycling has been around for more than 150 years, so it makes sense that it would be in the Olympics.

In 2008, BMX racing was added to the Olympics. BMX—bicycle motocross— is a type of off-road racing where the athletes do jumps around a tricky **track** with all kinds of twists and turns.

Women's BMX racing: Beijing 2008 Games

Track cycling is a race that goes round and round on a big track. The team sprint is like a relay race. A cyclist completes one lap, then pulls to the side so a teammate can take over. The team pursuit is a race with four teammates racing all at the same time. The track gets really crowded!

Road cycling is a longer race that goes on **paved** roads. These are usually endurance races. At the 2016 Summer Games, the gold medalist completed a 150-mile race in six hours and 10 minutes!

Mountain bike racing at the Olympics doesn't really happen on mountains. It takes place on a long, bumpy trail. The winning time in 2016 was one hour and 33 minutes.

Men's Cycling Mountain Bike: Rio de Janeiro 2016

Tennis

There are three kinds of tennis matches at the Olympics. Singles matches are one player vs. one player. Doubles matches are two vs. two. And mixed doubles feature one man and woman from the same country competing as a team against a man and woman from another country. Doubles teammates have to really work together well to win their match!

Men's tennis: Spain's Rafael Nadal

Steffi Graf

Tennis was part of the Olympics in 1896 but was dropped a few years later. It wasn't until 1988 that it returned as an official sport of the Games. That year, Germany's Steffi Graf won the gold medal. Graf would go on to become one of the best tennis players of all time.

DID YOU KNOW?

Leading up to the 2020 Games, athletes from the United States had earned more medals than athletes from any other country in the modern Summer Games.

1. United States: 2,522 medals.

2. Soviet Union: 1,010 medals

3. Great Britain: 847 medals.

4. France: 714 medals.

5. Germany: 615 medals.

Venus Williams (left) and Serena Williams (right)

American Venus Williams won a gold medal in 2000, and her sister Serena won gold in 2012. The Williams sisters have been almost unstoppable when they play together. Venus and Serena have won three gold medals in doubles Olympic tennis. Venus has five Olympic medals, tied for the most all-time in tennis.

"Every Olympics is something special," Venus said. "It's truly amazing."

United States tennis players have taken the most gold medals, but Great Britain has produced the most medal winners overall in tennis.

Archery and Shooting

Archery—the sport of using a bow and arrow—features four events: men's individual, women's individual, men's team and women's team. The distance from the archer to the target is 70 meters (230 feet). That's a really long shot!

Women's individual archery: Canada's Georcy-Stéphanie Picard (center)

Men's individual
archery

Each archer shoots 72 arrows. The closer they get to the bulls' eye, the more points they get. Whoever has the most points at the end is the winner!

South Korean archers have proven to be the best in the world. Since 1984, they have won 23 gold medals, more than any other country.

Shooting sports have been in all but two Summer Games since 1896. Olympic shooters compete in six different programs: air pistol, air rifle, rapid-fire pistol, rifle three positions, skeet and trap.

Air guns are guns that shoot out objects with **compressed air**. The rapid-fire pistol features targets that turn to face the shooter, then turn away when the time is up. Competitors have to think fast, before the target turns away!

China's Pang Wei win's gold in Men's 10 meter shooting

The rifle three positions event requires competitors to shoot at their targets from three different positions. First, they put one knee on the ground and rest their elbow on their other knee. Next, they lay flat on their stomachs. Then, they shoot while standing up, with their bodies turned to the side.

It's really hard to be a good shooter in all three positions! It takes a lot of practice.

Shooting events require a lot of practice and skill.

Women's skeet shooting:
Great Britain's Amber Hill

In skeet shooting, two machines send two clay targets flying through the air at the same time. The athletes have to shoot the clay targets before they hit the ground. Trap shooting is similar except there's only one machine and one target, but the targets move faster and are farther away than in skeet shooting.

CHAPTER 4

COMBAT SPORTS AND WATER SPORTS

Men's taekwondo: Uzbekistan's Dmitriy
Shokin (left) and Iran's Amidi Omidi (right)

The Summer Games feature four **combat** sports: boxing, judo, taekwondo and wrestling. Even though the athletes are not really fighting each other, they are either wearing **protective** gear or following rules that keep them from getting hurt.

It looks really rough sometimes, but combat sports competitors respect each other and usually shake hands when the fight is over. Being a good sport is important in the Olympics.

Women have competed in wrestling since the 2004 Athens Games.

In boxing, two people throw punches at each other while wearing protective gloves. Judo is a martial art from Japan, while taekwondo is a martial art from Korea. In judo, the athletes try to grab, push and pull each other to the ground. In taekwondo, they use kicks and punches.

In Olympic wrestling, athletes use all kinds of moves to try to pin their opponent to the mat. It might look like they're just grabbing and throwing each other like crazy, but the athletes really work hard to perfect their moves.

Russia's Karelin (left) and USA's Gardner (right)

Rulon Gardner is a famous American Olympic wrestler. In the 2000 Olympics, he was matched up against Russian Aleksandr Karelin, who had not lost a match in 13 years. Shockingly, Gardner won!

"How do you beat an individual who hasn't been beaten in 13 years?" Gardner said. "With the help of others."

Water Sports

Summer is the time to get on the water! That's why rowing, canoeing and kayaking are part of the Summer Olympics.

There are all kinds of different rowing events. Some have one person in a canoe, some have two, and some have as many as eight! A team of rowers has to work together to go as fast as possible. If one person gets off the pace, the whole team slows down.

There are two kinds of canoeing and kayaking: slalom and sprint. In slalom, athletes have to paddle down rapidly moving water in the fastest time possible. In sprint, boaters go as fast as they can across flat, still water.

Men's single kayak: Great Britain's Liam Heath wins gold

Other Individual Olympic Sports

These Olympic sports might not get as much attention as the others, but they're still super-fun to watch.

Triathlon is a competition in three events back-to-back-to-back: swimming, cycling and running. Talk about tiring!

Sailing involves racing in sailboats of various sizes. Sailors have to steer their boats around obstacles to get to the finish line.

Equestrian is another word for horse riding. Horses and their riders compete in three categories: dressage, show jumping, and eventing.

Golf is one most popular sports in the world, but after being part of the Olympics in 1900 and 1904, it didn't return to the Olympics until 2016!

Fencing is sword fighting with protective gear so no one gets hurt. Athletes get points by touching their opponents with a sword.

The modern **pentathlon** was invented just for the Olympics back in 1912. It includes the five events of fencing, pistol shooting, swimming, horseback riding and running.

GLOSSARY

accomplished to be successful through practice or training

ancient of a time long ago

banned something that is not allowed

celebrity someone who is famous

ceremony a fancy or important celebration

chariot a horse-drawn vehicle

combat fighting

compressed air air that is forced into a place that it normally wouldn't fit

decade a period of 10 years

endurance being able to compete a long time

exception something that doesn't follow a pattern

international between two or more countries

medals metal disks awarded to an athlete

paved covered with concrete, like a sidewalk or street

protective something that keeps you safe from injury

relay a race when team members take turns

stamina the ability to compete for a long time

track a course made for bicycles or other vehicles or competitors

wreath leaves or vines arranged in a circle

FOR MORE INFORMATION

Books About Olympians

Biles, Simone. *Courage to Soar: A Body in Motion, a Life in Balance.* Zondervan, 2016.

Fishman, Jon M. *Michael Phelps* (Sports All-Stars). Lerner, 2017.

Leigh, Anna. *Aly Raisman, Athlete and Activist.* Lerner Publications, 2019.

Mortensen, Lori. *Simone Biles: Gymnastics Star.* Capstone Press, 2018.

Books About the Olympics

Christopher, Matt. *Great Moments in the Summer Olympics.* Little Brown Young Readers, 2012.

Herman, Gail. *What Are the Summer Olympics?* Penguin Young Readers, 2016.

Time-Life Editors. *The Olympics: Moments That Made History.* Time-Life. 2016

Places

Elite Athlete Training Center, Chula Vista, California. Training center for BMX, volleyball, soccer athletes.

National High Performance Center, Oklahoma City, Oklahoma. Olympics training for rowing and kayak events.

United States Olympic Training Center, Colorado Springs, Colorado. Flagship training center for Olympic athletes in swimming, cycling, gymnastics.

INDEX

ABOUT THE AUTHOR

Aaron Derr is a writer based just outside of Dallas, Texas. He has more than 15 years of experience as a writer and editor for magazines such as *Sports Illustrated for Kids*, *TIME for Kids*, and *Boys Life*. When he's not reading or writing, Aaron enjoys watching and playing sports, and doing pretty much anything with his wife and two kids.